HUMAN RIGHTS AT RISK

THE EXCESSIVE USE OF FORCE BY POLICE

by Kari Cornell

BrightPoint Press

San Diego, CA

an imprint of ReferencePoint Press, Inc.
Printed in the United States

For more information, contact:
BrightPoint Press
PO Box 27779
San Diego, CA 92198
www.BrightPointPress.com

LIBRARY OF CONGRESS CATALOGING-IN-PUBLICATION DATA

Names: Cornell, Kari A., author.
Title: The excessive use of force by police / by Kari Cornell.
Description: San Diego, CA: BrightPoint Press, [2025] | Series: Human rights at risk | Includes bibliographical references and index. | Audience: Grades 7-9
Identifiers: LCCN 2024004129 (print) | LCCN 2024004130 (eBook) | ISBN 9781678209346 (hardcover) | ISBN 9781678209353 (eBook)
Subjects: LCSH: Police brutality--United States--Juvenile literature. | Police brutality--United States--History--Juvenile literature. | Police ethics--United States--Juvenile literature. | Police abolition movement--United States--Juvenile literature.
Classification: LCC HV7936.P725 C67 2025 (print) | LCC HV7936.P725 (eBook) | DDC 363.2/3--dc23/eng/20240214
LC record available at https://lccn.loc.gov/2024004129
LC eBook record available at https://lccn.loc.gov/2024004130

CONTENTS

AT A GLANCE

- Police officers sometimes use force as part of their jobs. Excessive use of force is when officers use more force than is reasonably needed in a situation.
- Police officers have injured and killed people by using both nonlethal and lethal excessive force.
- Excessive force has been a problem in police departments across the United States.
- Black people are disproportionately affected by police use of excessive force, a result of a history of discrimination that dates back to the era of slavery.
- Incidents of excessive force that are caught on video increase the visibility of these incidents and can spur public outcry.

- The 2020 murder of George Floyd by police officer Derek Chauvin in Minneapolis, Minnesota, put a spotlight on police use of excessive force.

- Organizations such as the National Action Network (NAN) and the ACLU Justice Lab help people affected by police violence.

- Policing reforms include de-escalation training, limits on when officers can use certain types of force, and increased accountability for officers who break the rules.

"I CAN'T BREATHE"

It was just a trip to a corner store in Minneapolis, Minnesota. But it changed the world forever. On May 25, 2020, George Floyd stepped into a store to buy cigarettes. After he left, the clerk called the police. He said Floyd paid with a fake twenty-dollar bill. He also said Floyd seemed drunk.

Two police officers, Thomas Lane and J. Alexander Kueng, arrived at the scene. Lane got Floyd out of his car and

George Floyd became an icon of the struggle against police use of excessive force.

handcuffed him. Floyd was distressed. But he was not violent. The police tried to get Floyd into their car. Floyd said he was afraid of tight spaces. He told them he couldn't breathe.

Officers Derek Chauvin and Tou Thao arrived. Chauvin tried to get Floyd into the

People set up memorials for Floyd at the site where the arrest took place.

police car. Then he pulled Floyd out of the car. Floyd was face down on the pavement. Lane, Kueng, and Chauvin held Floyd to the ground with their knees. They applied pressure to his legs, torso, and neck.

Floyd said, "I can't breathe, man, please!"[1] His mouth started to bleed. The officers called the dispatcher to report an injury. It was later upgraded to an emergency. Chauvin kept his knee against Floyd's neck. Floyd repeated, "I can't breathe. Please, the knee in my neck. I can't breathe."[2]

The ambulance arrived. Chauvin still had his knee on Floyd's neck. But Floyd was no longer moving. An **emergency medical technician (EMT)** asked Chauvin to release Floyd. They loaded him

Floyd's death drew national attention to the problem of police violence, inspiring a new protest movement.

into the ambulance and left the scene. Within minutes, Floyd had a heart attack. He was soon pronounced dead.

DEFINITION OF EXCESSIVE USE OF FORCE

George Floyd died because the police used excessive force. This is when officers apply more physical force than is reasonably needed. On that street corner, all four officers broke rules about the use of force. If they had followed those rules, Floyd might still be alive.

CHAPTER ONE

WHAT IS EXCESSIVE FORCE?

Excessive use of force is not just a problem in Minneapolis. It affects people across the country. Excessive use of force violates human rights. It also violates constitutional rights. The Fourth Amendment to the US Constitution forbids unreasonable searches and seizures. It exists to ensure that people feel safe in their homes and cars. But it also protects a

Police officers in the United States are entrusted with a lot of power. Many people believe that officers abuse this power.

SANTA MONICA
POLICE
POLICE PARKING
ONLY
ELIAS
Santa Monica
POLICE
29

person's right to feel safe just walking down the street.

A police officer's job is to keep their community safe. When a person breaks laws, they threaten the safety of others. Police are called in to help. A police officer's goal is to restore peace quickly. Use of force is always a last option. But there are some cases when the use of force may be needed. Police may need to act in self-defense or they may need to protect others in the community.

STANDARD OF REASONABLENESS

There are guidelines for the use of force. These are called the standard of reasonableness. This standard is used to see if an officer's actions are excessive.

Events can happen fast during an arrest. Police must quickly make decisions about the use of force.

Under the standard, an officer can use the amount of force that is reasonable to a fair-minded person. Fair-minded means thoughtful and not emotional. As the event happens, officers must decide quickly if force should be used. This can be difficult.

WHAT TYPES OF FORCE ARE EXCESSIVE?

There are two types of force. These are nonlethal and lethal. Nonlethal force involves tools that are not designed to kill people. Yet these tools can still cause harm or even death. For example, Chauvin used a knee restraint on Floyd. This is considered a nonlethal way to restrain someone. But it was fatal in Floyd's case.

Nonlethal use of force also includes using handcuffs to restrain people. **Tasers** and chemical sprays are nonlethal force, too. Since 2010, police using Tasers have killed at least 500 people. Tear gas, rubber bullets, and sound devices are nonlethal methods of force. The batons police carry are nonlethal as well.

Lethal use of force involves guns. Shootings make up 96 percent of killings by police. A group called Mapping Police Violence tracks the use of force in the

United States. It found that police killed 1,251 people in 2022. Many people have died in high-profile police shootings. They include Walter Scott, Philando Castile, Jordan Edwards, and Laquan McDonald.

COMMUNITIES OF COLOR

An officer's duty to keep people safe includes everyone. But excessive force affects people of color at a much higher

Increasing Deaths

In the year after George Floyd was killed, the number of Black people killed by police increased. The *Washington Post* gathers data on deaths by police. The number of Black people killed by police in 2021 was 1,055. This was up from 999 in 2019 and 1,021 in 2020.

rate than white people. Black people are 13 percent of the US population. Yet 21 percent of people who come into contact with the police are Black. About 33 percent of those in prison are Black people. In 2017, the Brookings Institute reported that young Black men were three times more likely to be killed by police than young white men.

Historically, people in Black communities experience more police violence than those in white neighborhoods. In many cases, the police who patrol Black neighborhoods do not live in those communities. In 2020, only 8 percent of Minneapolis police lived in the city of Minneapolis.

According to Sam Sanchez, this makes a difference. Sanchez is a community

US POLICE KILLINGS, 2013–2023

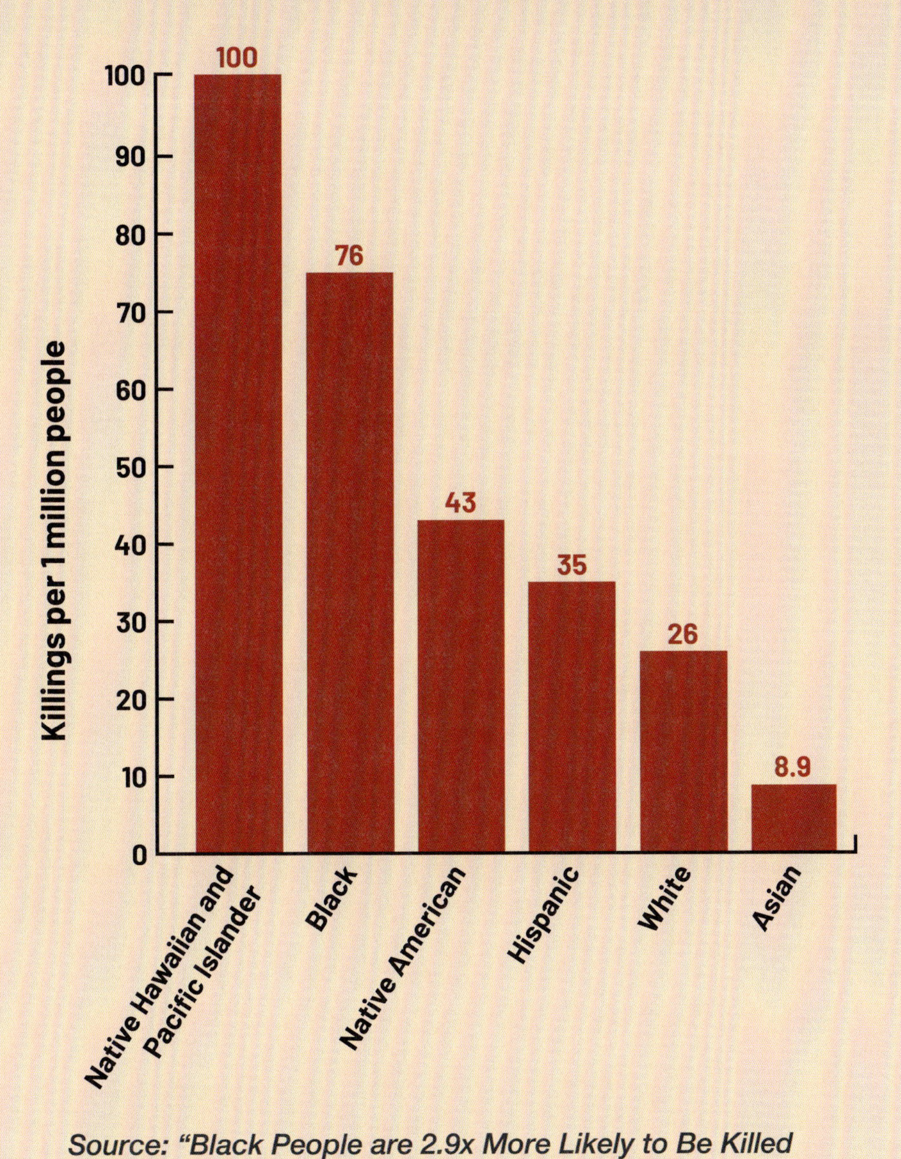

Source: "Black People are 2.9x More Likely to Be Killed by Police than White People in the US," Campaign Zero: Mapping Police Violence, *January 11, 2024. www.mappingpoliceviolence.org.*

The rate of Black people killed by police between 2013 and 2023 was far higher than the figure for white people.

Getting to know people in the community during events and block parties is one way police can build trust with those they serve.

organizer in Minnesota. He explains, "When a police officer lives in a community that they are supposed to serve, they're going to feel more accountable. They feel more ownership. They're going to have those community connections."[3] In other words, officers who live in the community where they work are more likely to treat people like neighbors.

The excessive use of force by police has deep roots in the United States. It goes back to early police departments controlling immigrants in cities. But it goes deeper than that. Modern policing also reflects the history of slavery and discrimination in the United States.

CHAPTER TWO

THE HISTORY OF EXCESSIVE FORCE

There's a sign on display at the National Museum of African American History and Culture. It reads, "We Demand an End to Police Brutality Now!"[4] This sign would have fit right in at the protests following the killing of George Floyd. But it's actually from a civil rights protest in 1963.

The history of excessive use of force by police stretches back even further than that.

People have been protesting about police use of excessive force for many decades.

Negroes Are Americans Too Protect Them
STOP BRUTALITY in ALABAMA
We Demand THE RIGHT TO VOTE EVERY-WHERE
We Demand

The methods that shape modern policing existed before there were police. Excessive force has its roots in slavery.

THE FIRST POLICE DEPARTMENTS

In the South, local patrols formed to help slave owners. These patrols tracked down runaway enslaved people. The first official slave patrol was in the Carolina colonies in 1704. This later served as a model for police departments.

The first official police department was formed in Boston, Massachusetts, in 1838. Northern US cities grew a lot during the 1800s. Nearly 30 million immigrants arrived from Europe. By the late 1880s, police departments existed in many cities. They helped control growing populations.

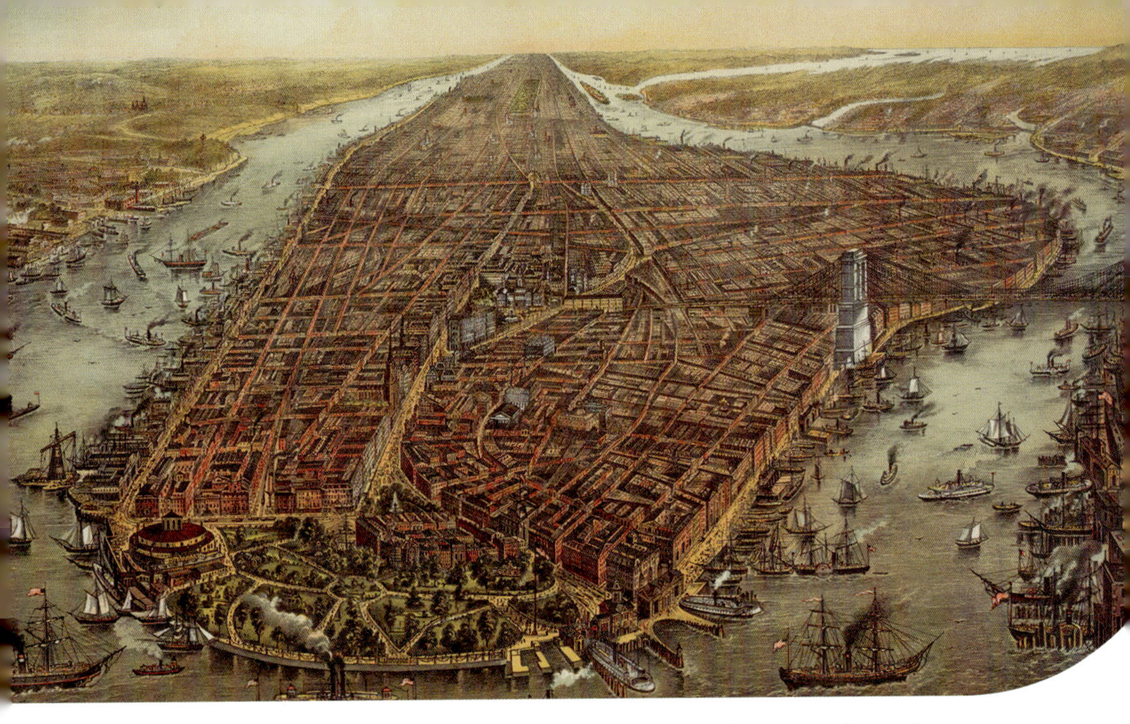

The growth of cities in the 1800s led to the creation of police departments to enforce the laws.

After the American Civil War (1861–1865), slavery was illegal. Yet local sheriffs still policed Black southerners harshly. They made sure people followed **segregation** laws.

FLEEING JIM CROW

By the late 1880s, Black people began to leave the South. They went to northern cities. They were trying to escape

Jim Crow laws. These laws required Black and white people to have separate public spaces. These were supposed to be equal. But spaces for Black people were worse than those for whites. People had to use

Legal segregation in the United States lasted into the 1960s in some places.

separate drinking fountains, bathrooms, and more.

Going north may have saved Black people from Jim Crow laws. But they still faced discrimination. Black people became targets for police brutality in northern cities.

In 1929 a survey tracked crime in Chicago, Illinois. Black people made up only 5 percent of the population. But 30 percent of those killed by police were Black.

CIVIL RIGHTS ERA

Discrimination continued in the South. On December 1, 1955, Rosa Parks took a stand. Parks was a Black woman. On that day she sat in the white section of a bus in Montgomery, Alabama. She refused to move to the back. This was where

Black people were supposed to sit. She was arrested.

Dr. Martin Luther King Jr. organized a bus **boycott** in the city. This was a form of protest. The boycott lasted for an entire year. In June 1956, a court ruled that bus segregation was unconstitutional. The city of Montgomery **desegregated** the buses. The Civil Rights Movement grew. During this time, a wave of protests broke out across the South.

The protests were largely peaceful. But police cracked down violently. They used dogs and fire hoses to control crowds. These protests appeared on the evening news. Those watching saw police use excessive force on protesters. Many of the protesters were Black people.

Americans were shocked to see the use of dogs against peaceful protesters on television news programs.

On July 12, 1967, a Black cab driver was pulled over by police in Newark, New Jersey. His name was John Smith. The population of Newark was more than 50 percent Black. But its police department was only 11 percent Black.

Police said Smith's license was not valid. They beat him brutally. Then they arrested him. Riots erupted in Newark. In 4 days, twenty-six people died.

CAUGHT ON FILM

Many other Black people have faced excessive force during traffic stops. On March 3, 1991, Rodney King tried to flee police in his car. Eventually he pulled over. Witnesses said he did not resist arrest. Yet police hit King with batons more than fifty times. They also tased and kicked him. King suffered a broken leg and bruises. Bystander George Holliday captured the beating on video.

In April 1992, the officers were put on trial. They were Laurence Powell,

Timothy Wind, Theodore Briseno, and Stacey Koon. All four were found not guilty. When the verdict was announced, riots erupted across Los Angeles. More than 2,000 were injured, and fifty-five people died.

In 2022, people commemorated the thirtieth anniversary of the 1992 Los Angeles riots.

Incidents like these have played out again and again. Advancing technology has helped news of such incidents reach a larger audience. On July 6, 2016, Philando Castile was shot by police in Minnesota. It was a routine traffic stop for broken brake lights. Castile informed the officer that he had a gun. Then he reached for his wallet. The officer shot him.

Breonna Taylor

Weeks before George Floyd's murder, police were investigating a drug deal in Louisville, Kentucky. They knocked on Breonna Taylor's door. Taylor's boyfriend, Kenneth Walker, said they were not in uniform. They did not say they were police. Walker fired a warning shot at the unknown intruders. They forced their way in and fired thirty-two shots. Taylor was killed.

Castile's fiancée, Diamond Reynolds, was in the seat next to him. She live streamed what happened after the shooting. Then she posted it to Facebook. People around the world watched the video. Protests broke out across the nation. Officer Jeronimo Yanez was charged in the death. He was found not guilty. But he was fired from his job.

The arrest of George Floyd was also captured on video. Darnella Frazier recorded the incident on her smartphone. Video footage has helped spread awareness. Today many people and organizations are working to reduce the excessive use of force by police.

CHAPTER THREE

ORGANIZATIONS AGAINST EXCESSIVE FORCE

George Floyd's death inspired people to act. Many civil rights organizations are working to end excessive use of force. Some of these organizations have been around for a long time. These include local chapters of the National Association for the Advancement of Colored People (NAACP). The NAACP has called for police to be held accountable for their actions.

The NAACP is one of the longest-running civil rights groups.

NAACP
TO ENSURE

Other groups formed more recently. The ACLU Justice Lab helps victims of excessive force. It formed in June 2020 in response to Floyd's killing. Organizations working on this issue also include the National Action Network (NAN), Black Lives Matter (BLM), and Amnesty International.

NATIONAL ACTION NETWORK

Reverend Al Sharpton formed NAN in 1991. The organization is inspired by Martin Luther King Jr. It fights for equal rights and justice for all. NAN has worked to pass laws against racial profiling. This is when police stop people just because of their race. In the 1990s, this method of policing was common. With the help of NAN, it is now used less frequently.

Reverend Al Sharpton has been a civil rights activist since the 1970s.

NAN is also working to hold police accountable. In New York it helped create a new rule. A special lawyer must be assigned to all cases where police shoot an unarmed person. NAN has worked to pass this policy across the country. A similar order was passed in California in 2017. The organization has also fought for police officers to wear body cameras.

ACLU JUSTICE LAB

The ACLU Justice Lab is based in New Orleans, Louisiana. It is the first program of its kind in the United States. Its goal is to challenge biased policing. Justice Lab provides lawyers to those who have faced police violence because of their race.

Justice Lab works with law firms and legal clinics at law schools. It defends people whose Fourth Amendment rights were violated. It take cases involving excessive force, racial profiling, and unreasonable stops.

NAACP

The NAACP was formed in Springfield, Illinois in 1909, after the Springfield Race Riot. In this incident, white people attacked the town's Black community. They were upset when a Black man who was wrongly accused of rape was

Ending racial profiling has been one focus of the NAACP.

transported out of town. The NAACP's founding members were W. E. B. Du Bois and Ida Bell Wells-Barnett. They wanted to tackle challenges Black Americans faced. Excessive use of force is one of these challenges.

The group has pushed for laws to stop racial profiling. The NAACP has also worked to set up civilian complaint review boards. These are groups of everyday citizens who look into complaints about police officers. The NAACP has also pushed for a national database to track police violence.

BLACK LIVES MATTER

Trayvon Martin was 17 years old when he died in Sanford, Florida. He was killed on February 26, 2012. Martin was shot by local

In the wake of Trayvon Martin's death, protesters took to the streets to call for justice.

man George Zimmerman. Zimmerman shot Martin because he thought he looked suspicious. When Zimmerman was found not guilty in 2013, three women took action. Alicia Garza, Patrisse Cullors, and Opal Tometi were tired of seeing Black men die. They founded Black Lives Matter to do something about it.

At first BLM was just a hashtag. The founders posted it on social media in response to Martin's death. Then #blacklivesmatter became a movement across the country. BLM chapters protested the loss of Black lives, including those killed by police. Their mission is to end white supremacy, the belief that white people are superior to people of color. BLM works to prevent police and **vigilante** violence

Bills for Black Lives

BLM supporters in New Jersey tried to pass bills against police brutality in 2022. One bill outlawed chokeholds. Another established review boards to record police behavior. A third made police discipline records public. And a fourth ended qualified immunity in some cases. These bills did not pass.

against Black communities. The group aims to make policing more transparent. It supports building trust between police and communities.

Cofounder Garza believes building this trust is possible. She says that change must begin locally. This is why she started BLM. "You have to believe that change can happen if you are going to be a part of making change," Garza explained.[5]

AMNESTY INTERNATIONAL

Amnesty International is a global organization that fights human rights violations. Part of its mission is to stop excessive use of force. Amnesty International aims to hold police accountable for unlawful deaths.

One way to do this is through research. After Floyd was killed, Amnesty International observers went to BLM protests. They counted 125 incidents of alleged police

Amnesty International works on a wide range of human rights issues.

violence against protestors, journalists, medics, and legal observers between May and June 2020. These events happened in forty states and in Washington, DC. Police used batons, rubber bullets, tear gas, and pepper spray to control people at protests.

Amnesty International uses its research to make change. It presents the findings to governments and companies. Then it asks these organizations to create new laws and policies to change things for the better.

CHAPTER FOUR

POLICE REFORM

In the wake of George Floyd's death, protesters called for justice. Eventually, all four officers were found guilty. Derek Chauvin was convicted of second- and third-degree murder. He was also convicted of second-degree **manslaughter**. The state of Minnesota sentenced Chauvin to 22.5 years in prison. The federal government sentenced him to 21 years

Many protesters agreed with the Chauvin verdict but also demanded wider reforms about police violence.

CHAUVIN IS GUILTY
BUT SO IS THE
SYSTEM
#ABOLISH

in prison. He is serving both sentences at the same time.

The three other officers were also found guilty. Tou Thao was sentenced to 4 years and 9 months in prison by the state and 3.5 years by the federal government. Thomas Lane was sentenced to 2.5 years in prison by the federal government and 3 years by the state. J. Alexander Kueng was sentenced to 3 years in prison by the federal government while the state sentenced him to 3.5 years. Convictions such as these are rare.

FROM GRIEF TO ACTION

On April 12, 2023, NAN organized a panel. Families of George Floyd, Eric Garner, Tyre Nichols, and others met in

Vice President Kamala Harris was among the speakers at the April 2023 NAN event in New York.

New York. All spoke about the effect police violence has had on their lives. They talked about their loved ones. Then the families discussed police reform.

The night before the panel, the city of Memphis, Tennessee, passed the Driving Equality Act in honor of Tyre Nichols. The **ordinance** bans police from stopping drivers for small issues like broken lights.

Nichols was pulled over by police in Memphis on January 7, 2023. Officers said he was driving recklessly. Police tased, kicked, punched, and beat Nichols. He died 3 days later. Row Vaughn was Nichols's mother. She said, "We are going to continue to fight so that this doesn't happen to

Garner's mother, Gwen Carr (center), attended the signing of the Eric Garner Anti-Chokehold Act in Harlem in June 2020.

another Tyre. There's just too many of our Black men being killed for nothing."[6]

Eric Garner died as police were arresting him on July 17, 2014, on Staten Island, New York. They put him in a chokehold and wrestled him to the ground. Garner's last words were "I can't breathe."[7]

Gwen Carr is the mother of Eric Garner. In 2020, Carr helped pass the Eric Garner Anti-Chokehold Act in New York. Under this bill, officers who kill or harm a person using a chokehold can be charged with a felony. They may receive up to 15 years in prison. Passing this bill wasn't easy, but Carr knew she had to do something. Carr said, "I remember when this horrible incident happened to my son. I didn't know what I would do. I was in a dark place at that time. But I decided to turn my mourning into action."[8]

MINNEAPOLIS REFORMS

The state of Minnesota investigated Floyd's death in 2022. Officials and activists wanted to make sure nothing like this ever happened again. But change is hard. Rebecca Lucero is the commissioner for the Minneapolis Department of Human Rights (MDHR). She said, "It is going to take all of us . . . to tackle the structural, transformational shifts that must happen for lasting change to occur."[9]

Plans for police reform include rules for use of force. They require officers to **de-escalate**. The rules prohibit officers from using force to punish or retaliate.

Building stronger connections between police and communities is one possible way to reduce excessive use of force.

They prohibit some minor traffic stops. Rules also ban searches based on smells of cannabis. They prohibit consent searches during pedestrian or vehicle stops. This is a search by police that a person has agreed to allow. These rules limit when officers can use force. And they limit when officers can use chemical sprays and Tasers.

MDHR hopes to end **military-like training**. It aims to increase police accountability. And it hopes to push leaders to resolve racial disparities.

REFORM IN OTHER CITIES

Amnesty International reports that nine US states have no laws limiting excessive force.

CAHOOTS

The city of Eugene, Oregon, started its Crisis Assistance Helping Out on the Streets (CAHOOTS) program in the 1990s. Crisis workers and medics work in teams to help those experiencing a mental health crisis. They provide emergency medical care, counseling, and transportation. Many cities have based their mental health response teams on the CAHOOTS model.

Since 2020, communities have been trying to change this. Human rights groups have provided guidelines.

Some states have passed laws that set guidelines around the use of force. Some require officers to report when another officer breaks those rules. And they create policies to punish police. These policies can prevent people from returning to the police force.

CHANGE FOR GOOD

A 2020 study looked at 911 calls in eight cities. Between 21 and 38 percent of calls were about drug use, homelessness, and mental health issues. In these cases, mental health professionals may be a better option than police.

Communities are changing the response to these types of calls. In San Francisco, California, special teams respond to mental health calls. They do not include police.

In Austin, Texas, officials moved funding from police to community programs.

Improving police training for responses to mental health crises is one way to reduce the excessive use of force.

They help people facing substance abuse, mental illness, or homelessness.

Community violence prevention programs can also help. Northside Residents Redevelopment Council (NRRC) formed in Minneapolis. When violence escalated, block leaders kept watch. They worked with activists to prevent violence.

These are just a few possible solutions. Policing has a history of excessive force and discrimination. These are still major problems today. Changing these patterns will take time. People and organizations are working to end the excessive use of force by police.

GLOSSARY

boycott
to refuse to do something or use a service as an act of protest

de-escalate
to reduce tensions

desegregate
to be free of laws requiring races to be separated

Emergency Medical Technicians (EMTs)
medical workers who care for people at the scene of an accident

manslaughter
the act of killing a person without intent or the desire to harm them

military-like training
a type of training that approaches policing like going to war

ordinance
a piece of legislation passed by a government body

qualified immunity
a protection that prevents a police officer from being tried for violating a person's human rights

segregation
the separation of races by neighborhood or in public spaces

Taser
a gun that fires an electrical charge

vigilante
a person or group who punishes someone on their own authority

SOURCE NOTES

INTRODUCTION: "I CAN'T BREATHE"

1. Evan Hill, Ainara Tiefenthaler, et al. "How George Floyd Was Killed in Police Custody," *New York Times*, May 31, 2020. www.nytimes.com.

2. Evan Hill, Ainara Tiefenthaler, et al. "How George Floyd Was Killed in Police Custody."

CHAPTER ONE: WHAT IS EXCESSIVE FORCE?

3. Libor Jany. "Only About 8 Percent of Minneapolis Police Officers Live in City Limits," *Star Tribune*, August 24, 2017. www.startribune.com.

CHAPTER TWO: THE HISTORY OF EXCESSIVE FORCE

4. Nodjimbadem, Katie. "The Long, Painful History of Police Brutality in the U.S.," *Smithsonian Magazine*, Updated: May 29, 2020. www.smithsonianmag.com.

CHAPTER THREE: ORGANIZATIONS AGAINST EXCESSIVE FORCE

5. Marianne Schnall, "Interview with #BlackLivesMatter Cofounder Alicia Garza: 'Fight Against Despair and Keep Doing the Work Needed to Change the World," *Forbes*, January 15, 2021. www.forbes.com.

CHAPTER FOUR: POLICE REFORM

6. Kiara Alfonseca, "Families of Police Brutality Victims Gather to Turn 'Grief into Action,'" *ABC News*, April 12, 2023. www.abcnews.go.com.

7. Al Baker, J. David Goodman, and Benjamin Mueller, "Beyond the Chokehold: The Path to Eric Garner's Death," *New York Times,* June 13, 2015. www.nytimes.com.

9. Andi Babineau and David J. Lopez, "Minneapolis Agrees to Policing Plan Overhaul Forged After George Floyd's Killing," *CNN*, April 1, 2023. www.cnn.com.

FOR FURTHER RESEARCH

BOOKS

Jim Gallagher, *Policing and Race: The Debate over Excessive Use of Force*. San Diego, CA: ReferencePoint Press, 2021.

Duchess Harris and Alexis Burling, *The Killing of George Floyd*. Minneapolis, MN: Abdo, 2021.

Philip Wolny, *The Police and Excessive Use of Force*. San Diego, CA: BrightPoint Press, 2021.

INTERNET SOURCES

Evan Hill, Ainara Tiefenthäler, et al., "How George Floyd Was Killed in Police Custody," *New York Times*, May 31, 2020. www.nytimes.com.

Katie Nodjimbadem, "The Long, Painful History of Police Brutality in the US," *Smithsonian Magazine*, May 29, 2020. www.smithsonianmag.com.

Aja Beckham, "Teen Authors from DC Reflect on Police Brutality, Racial Justice in 2020 Children's Books," *WAMU 88.5: American University Radio*, November 24, 2020. www.wamu.org.

WEBSITES

Amnesty International: Police Violence
www.amnesty.org/en/what-we-do/police-brutality

The website of Amnesty International includes information about the use of excessive force by police in the United States and around the world.

Council for a Strong America: Youth Police Interactions
www.strongnation.org/topics/youth-police-interactions

The Youth Police Interactions site features articles about how police officers and departments are working to connect with youth in their communities. Many of the stories involve programs that help officers understand the issues youth are struggling with in their daily lives.

Police Brutality in the United States
www.kids.britannica.com/students/article/police-brutality-in-the-United-States/632497

Britannica's website explains what police brutality is and provides examples. It also gives a history of excessive use of force by police and talks about the different groups that have been affected by it.

INDEX

IMAGE CREDITS

Cover: © Sheila Fitzgerald/Alamy
5: © Hayk_Shalunts/Shutterstock Images
7: © Ben Von Klemperer/Shutterstock Images
8: © Ben Harding/Shutterstock Images
10: © Ron Adar/Shutterstock Images
13: © Adolf Martinez Soler/Shutterstock Images
15: © Ron Adar/Shutterstock Images
19: © Red Line Editorial
20: © Steven J. Hensley/Shutterstock Images
23: © Warren K. Leffler/Library of Congress
25: © George Schlegel/Library of Congress
26: © Everett Collection/Shutterstock Images
29: © Bill Hudson/AP Images
31: © Ringo Chiu/Shutterstock Images
35: © Robert P. Alvarez/Shutterstock Images
37: © Lev Radin/Shutterstock Images
39: © rblfmr/Shutterstock Images
41: © Ira Bostic/Shutterstock Images
44: © Shawn Goldberg/Shutterstock Images
47: © Ron Adar/Shutterstock Images
49: © Steve Sanchez Photos/Shutterstock Images
50: © Kevin RC Wilson/Shutterstock Images
53: © Jelani Photography/Shutterstock Images
56: © Ground Picture/Shutterstock Images

ABOUT THE AUTHOR

Kari Cornell is an award-winning children's book author who gardens, runs, and makes pottery. She lives in Minneapolis with her husband, two boys, and their sweet dog, EmmyLou.